Hilary,

I hope you enjoy this little book as much as I did. Keep it forever and look at it when your feeling blue. Always know I love you & your brother more than life. I am, and will always be there for you. I wish you love, laughter, music & happiness because you are a beautiful, smart & talented young lady.

Love always
Mom

The Two of Us

The TWO of US

A Book About Mothers and Daughters

By Ellen Small and Sara Schapiro

**Andrews McMeel
Publishing**

Kansas City

The Two of Us

02 03 04 05 06 CTP 10 9 8 7 6 5 4 3 2 1

ISBN: 0-7407-2243-3

Library of Congress Catalog Card Number: 2001053472

Book design by Holly Camerlinck

Attention: Schools and Businesses

Andrews McMeel books are available at quantity discounts with bulk purchase
for educational, business, or sales promotional use. For information, please write to:
Special Sales Department, Andrews McMeel Publishing,
4520 Main Street, Kansas City, Missouri 64111.

The two of us...

... have loved each other
since the moment we met.

. . . can share each other's company without talking.

. . . could pass for sisters
(if it weren't for one of us having
a few more wrinkles).

... never like the way we look
in family photographs (but always like
the way the other one looks).

. . . don't like to be in different places on holidays.

. . . love a good shoe sale

(as if there's such a thing as a "bad" shoe sale).

. . . are always in search of the perfect
black purse.

. . . have the same taste in clothes
(but would never wear
mother-daughter outfits).

The two of us . . .

. . . have been known to "borrow"
each other's clothes.

Well almost!!!

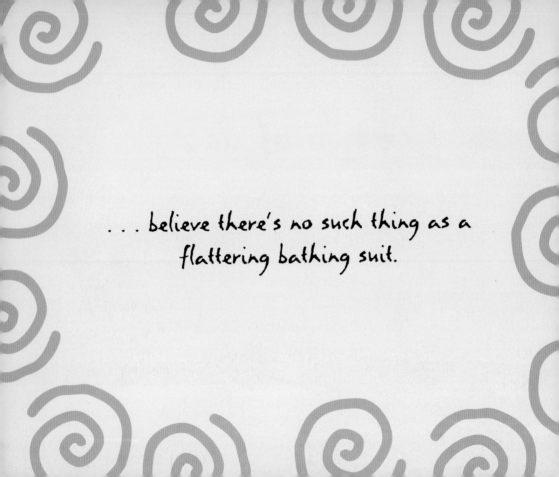

. . . believe there's no such thing as a flattering bathing suit.

. . . speak in Mother-Daughter Shorthand.

. . . have almost the exact same color hair

(thanks to hair dye).

. . . like the same books and movies
but hate each other's music.

2nd one "not" true

. . . have the same taste in men
(give or take twenty-five years).

. . . admit we're low-tech and
high-maintenance.

. . . exist on low-calorie, low-fat, low-sugar everything (and then reward ourselves with real Coke and M&M's).

. . . sometimes get tired of arugula and radicchio salads and have greasy cheeseburgers and fries.

. . . use the exercise bike to dry panty hose.

. . . have a love-hate relationship
with exercise: We love the idea.
We hate doing it.

. . . have the same:

voice (and like to see how long
it takes people who call to figure out
they're not talking to who they think
they're talking to).

signature (from years of one of us
forging report cards).

. . . like to dance at family events
(usually with each other).

. . . are keeping up the tradition of
passing down family recipes

(except certain bad dishes, which we
have taken it upon ourselves to weed out
for the family's own good).

The two of us . . .

. . . love mall shopping, catalog shopping, on-line shopping (okay, just shopping).

. . . would rather spend money on a coat than a boat.

. . . gossip about people we don't know,
especially movie stars.

. . . fight over the new issue of
People magazine.

. . . are addicted to sleazy TV talk shows
(but are embarrassed to admit it).

. . . know that (<u>female star</u>) once dated
(<u>male pro athlete</u>) but has a child
by (<u>rock star</u>).

. . . love cooking shows
(more than we love actually cooking).

. . . watch plastic surgery specials on cable.

. . . can't stand to see:

baseball players spit tobacco.

stock car racing.

old guys in Speedos.

. . . are hooked on old movies,
especially old romantic comedies.

. . . cry at the same happy and sad endings.

. . . can figure out whodunit
before he even dunit.

. . . have been known to sneak our own
candy into movie theaters.

The two of us . . .

. . . are each other's worst critic
and biggest fan.

. . . have the same perfect bodies—
except for our 1) thighs 2) hips
3) feet 4) boobs . . .

. . . would rather sleep in a soft,
old, torn T-shirt than a
Victoria's Secret negligee.

. . . always overpack for vacations
and then wear
the same three things.

. . . don't always have exactly the same definition of "neat" (since one of us used to hide her dirty laundry under her bed).

. . . have our own secret words
for bodily functions.

. . . signal each other if there's
food in our teeth.

. . . could order each other's exact meal
in a restaurant.

. . . will drink out of the same glass, eat off the same fork, even lick the same ice cream cone—but no one else's!

. . . like to have a cup of ~~tea~~ milk together
(preferably with a couple of cookies
on the side).

. . . never have enough time together.

I miss you so . . .

. . . both like to collect stuff—
teacups, old books, wooden toys,
spoons, glass bottles, deco jewelry . . .

. . . love to pore over old family albums and complain about how stupid our hair looked, how ugly our clothes were, and how thin we used to be.

The two of us . . .

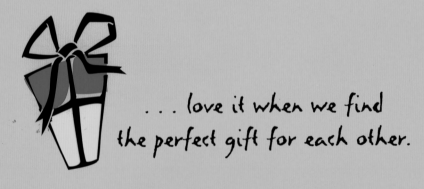

. . . love it when we find
the perfect gift for each other.

. . . don't know how to say "no"
to each other.

←

. . . think each other is almost perfect
(since most traits are inherited). OK, we are perfect

⇒

. . . are the smartest women we know
(but we don't flaunt it).

. . . would call each other as lifelines on
Who Wants to Be a Millionaire.

. . . eat chocolate baking chips
right out of the bag while making cookies
(and eat the dough raw, too,
then wonder why the recipe didn't
make as many cookies as it should).

. . . can make each other laugh
so hard we feel like we might
have a little "accident."

Won't forget the Post-man
& the phrase "right on" has a
new meaning!!!

ha•o

. . . wear elastic-waisted pants to holiday dinners so we can eat more.

. . . don't hold back at the buffet line.

. . . are even alike when we try not to be.

. . . have the same mannerisms.
(Now, how did that happen?)

. . . are usually on the same wavelength
when it comes to:

politics

men

fashion

The two of us . . .

. . . both own miniskirts,
one from this season, one from 1972.

. . . both have pierced ears
(but one of us has one hole per ear;
the other has a few extra).

. . . sometimes get mad at each other
but get over it quickly.

. . . have already planned the perfect wedding (even if there's no date, no ring, and no groom yet).

. . . know just how the other one
would feel about something even when
one of us isn't there.

. . . don't always take each other's advice
but then later wish we had.

. . . take care of each other when we're sick.

. . . think fathers and sons are great
but not as cool as mothers and daughters.

The two of us . . .

. . . are living proof there's something
to this genetics stuff.

. . . have learned a lot from each other.

. . . are sometimes away from each other
but never far apart.

And if we could choose from all the people in the world, the two of us would pick each other as mother and daughter.

God blessed me when he gave me you
I am proud of you & love you more
than life...